8/82

I0566436

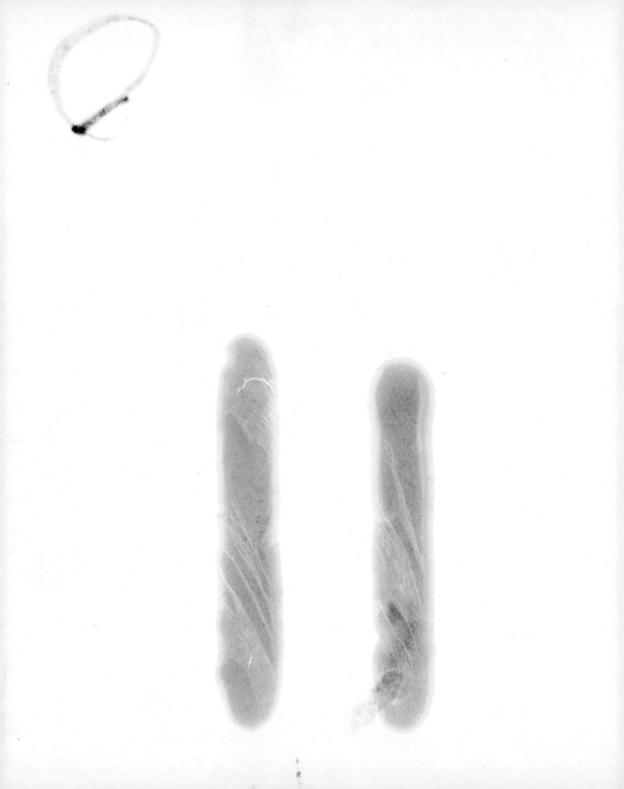

FOLK COSTUME
OF WESTERN EUROPE

*"Pen-sardin" or Sardine Cap, from
the sardine fisheries of Finisterre, Brittany*

Couple from Ärstad in Halland, Sweden

Opposite:
Jewelled silver cross
of Normandy

FOLK COSTUME
OF WESTERN EUROPE

LILLA M. FOX

Illustrated by the author

PLAYS, INC.

Folk costume of Denmark

Contents

*Going to evening service
in Hesse, Germany*

*Headdress and clog
of Staphorst, Holland*

Tara brooch

Laplander

Irish dancer

Boy of Hesse in Germany

Introduction

Although nowadays people dress in much the same kind of clothes all over Europe, not long ago the traveller could see costumes which varied from district to district—in the mountains, from valley to valley, and in some places, like Sweden, from village to village. There were (and still are) different dresses for Sundays, for christenings or weddings or funerals, and for the feast-days, such as Christmas and Midsummer.

The oldest and simplest costume was made up of some sort of tunic and leg-coverings, with leather shoes and a cloak of skin for the coldest weather. The people of Lapland in northern Scandinavia still wear this clothing, men and women alike, although they have added details of later fashions, decorating the tunics with braiding and using zip fasteners. In ancient Ireland peasants often wore a length of material round their waists, called a *kelt*. The *kelt* or kilt is now tailored and is

7

still worn by some Irishmen as well as by the Scots. An old type of tunic was the Saxon *smoca*, from which came the English smock and the blue working-blouses still worn in France, the Low Countries and parts of Germany.

These ancient garments changed slowly. Some country places were so remote that the people rarely saw other styles of dress. The garments were made from hand-spun and hand-woven material, heavy and long-lasting, were handed down from parents to children, and finally were cut up for the little ones. The special clothes worn on Sundays and feast-days were decorated and embroidered and were handed down for several generations.

However, clothes did of course change. Sometimes conquerors brought new styles; wealthier people wore new fashions, and the peasants copied the parts they liked; merchants brought new materials; sailors and soldiers brought clothes and jewellery and rare materials from abroad. Lace-making began in Italy and Flanders about six hundred years ago and spread over Europe, many regions inventing their own patterns. Women started to wear the Italian fashion of

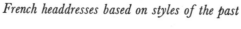

French headdresses based on styles of the past

French hood of High Savoy

Tower of Normandy

Lace cap of Auvergne

Dutch fisherwomen's everyday dress, Scheveningen

laced bodices over a white chemise (shift) and full skirts instead of the old loose gown. When the western countries discovered India, Indian shawls became fashionable; later, they were made cheaply in factories and were adopted by most peasant women. At about the same time, men took to wearing jackets or coats and coloured waistcoats with many buttons, and breeches instead of the old baggy trousers seen on page 18.

So different styles and details were adopted and adapted into this costume and that, and the result is a great variety of costumes, some made up of a great variety of fashions.

There are only a few places left in western Europe where folk costume is worn every day; and a few more where it is worn for Sundays and special occasions. It is more often worn by women, since many old customs to do with home life are kept alive by the women rather than by the men. In Scheveningen in the Netherlands, the fisherwomen still wear their folk costume for work, even though their little fishing village is now part of a big holiday resort.

Folk costume is also worn by folk-dancing groups, who are very careful to get it right and not to wear the costume of one district for the dances of another. Who would dream of dancing a Highland Fling in a smock! Anyone producing plays or dances that need folk costume should try to make the costume as like as possible to that of the region concerned. There are many more folk costumes than there is room for in this book; but other books can be looked at and advice asked from tourist agencies or from the English Folk Dance and Song Society. People should avoid mixing the regional costumes of any country and calling the result "national" dress. To do this is as absurd as dressing someone in a kilt, a Pearly King's jacket and Lancashire clogs and calling the mixture British national costume.

Folk costume of the Odenwald mountains of south Germany and the Baltic island of Rügen

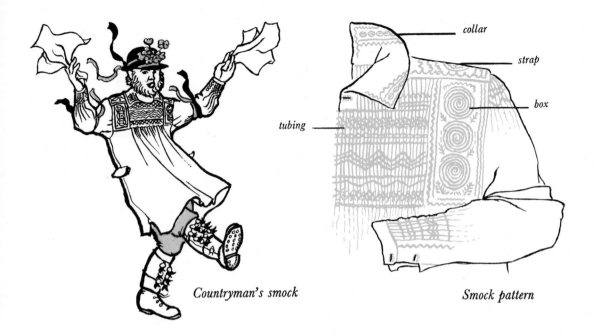

Countryman's smock

collar
strap
box
tubing

Smock pattern

1 Great Britain

England Here we have one of the oldest and two of the newest folk costumes in Europe. The oldest is the smock, which started as a shapeless tunic worn by peasants in very early times. Later it was gathered at the shoulders, yoke, and wrists by the stretchable embroidery called smocking. It was strong and showerproof, and its colour was whiteybrown or blue or green, according to the part of England in which it was worn. Sunday smocks were white. It was a practical garment, especially for dairy work, as it was washable. In Berkshire it was called a cow gown. Sometimes the embroidery on the collar, or on the "boxes" (panels on either side of the front fastening) showed the trade of the wearer—flowers for a gardener, or crooks for a shepherd—so that farmers could "read" the smocks of the workers waiting to be hired at "hiring" fairs. The patterns of smocks also varied from place to place, as did the knitting patterns of fishermen's blue jerseys, which the fishermen knitted themselves, so that those who knew could tell where the wearer came from.

England was the first country to have heavy industry, and in the North Country mills and factories the women's shawls and long, full skirts became so generally worn that they can be called a folk costume. It was a practical costume, keeping out rain and cold. People wore clogs with wooden soles, to which the uppers were nailed with studs; the heels had horse-shoe shaped clog-irons which clattered over the cobbles.

North country working girl

Coster holiday dress

Lancashire clog

Morris dancer from Berkshire

Sword dancer of Yorkshire

Bacup coconut dancer of Lancashire

The latest folk costume is that of the Pearlies, the costermongers of London. The costermongers (costermonger means apple-seller) used to bring round apples and other fruit and vegetables in little pony-carts, and were very much part of London life not long ago. They sewed mother-of-pearl buttons and shapes on to their clothes and the women wore big feathered hats.

English folk dancers wear various costumes that are the traditional wear for certain dances, some of which are illustrated.

13

Gwent

Pembrokeshire

Llanberis

Wales In Wales, as in other remote mountainous places, ways changed more slowly, and up to the end of the last century folk costumes were everyday wear for many country and fishing people, especially for the women, who wore full skirts and fitting bodices, aprons and small shawls or kerchiefs. The Pembrokeshire costume has separate sleeves that tie on at the shoulders, as in some Elizabethan country dresses. Large hats were worn over lace caps, and each district had its own style. The hat from Gwent is like that of seventeenth-century Puritans; the Pembrokeshire hat is a topper, like the men's; and the Llanberis townswoman's hat is very tall.

14

Ireland For many centuries before she was sacked by the Vikings, Ireland had a rich civilisation of her own. Some of the clothes worn then, such as the *kelt*, the wide mantle, and the leather shoes called *brogs*, have a modern form. Garments were often dyed yellow with saffron, and the saffron kilt is still worn by some Irish regiments and by folk dancers. The mantle is fastened with a silver Tara brooch, like old Celtic *fibula*.

Ireland was invaded many times, and the peasants adopted some of the fashions of their conquerors. Until a little while ago Connemara women wore shawls with richly patterned edges, and in Munster women wore large hoods of Moorish origin.

Unfortunately, few of the old folk costumes survive, and on the stage Irishmen are often dressed instead in a comic version of the Sunday clothes worn by peasants about a hundred years ago. These were a jacket and breeches, usually green, for the men, and a dress, also green, for the girls, with the skirt looped up to show the red under-kirtle.

Connemara boy

Connemara shawl, Galway
Munster hood

Irish country dance costume

Highland trews first worn for riding

Seaweed gatherer of the Island of Skye

Highland woman with plaid

Scottish plaid draped and belted

Fishwife's best dress, Newhaven

Costume still worn for Highland dancing

Scotland According to the Romans, the Highlanders of Scotland also wore the *kelt* and went bare-legged and bare-footed as the Irish warriors did. Later they wore the "Great Plaid", a length of material folded into pleats round the waist, with enough to overlap at the front and with a long end to throw over the shoulder; it was held in place by a belt from which hung a deerskin purse called a sporran. Later this was made into two garments, the pleated kilt and the plaid, which was both overcoat and sleeping-bag to the Highlander. The material was woven in colours which varied from place to place, and was called tartan. The clan chiefs could dress their followers in a particular colour pattern or "set", and in time each clan had its own tartan.

Lowland dress was much like that of England except for some fisher-folk's. The Newhaven fishwife opposite wears a costume with a finely pleated skirt and a hanging pocket, as in Scandinavia. There is a strong link with Scandinavia—along the east coasts and in the Shetlands and Orkneys, where the Vikings settled. The art of knitting which we call "Fair Isle" was brought to those islands from Telemark in Norway. This knitting is now world-famous and can be very expensive to buy. Scottish fisher-lasses, however, often wear the most beautiful Fair Isle jerseys for workaday tasks, such as gutting herrings.

Some traditional Fair Isle patterns

2 France

France is a country made up from many old kingdoms, some mountain-ous, others with farmland and vineyards. It is also a country of many races, from the small, dark people near the Mediterranean Sea to the tall natives of Normandy in the North. The old kingdoms, now prov-inces, have kept some of their own ways and character, although they have long since joined to become one nation.

This is most true of Brittany, a rocky, windswept region where the people, hardy fishermen and farmers, are of the same stock as the Welsh and Cornishmen of Great Britain. The everyday language, Breton, is like enough to Welsh for the two peoples to be able to talk together. Brittany is rich in legends, customs, traditional music and costumes. Breton lace-makers have become famous and feast-day garments are rich with lace.

Working clothes in the town of Quimper were baggy white linen trousers (called *bragon bas*) with a wide belt, gaiters and wooden *sabots* (clogs), a round-necked blue jacket, a full shirt, and sometimes a sleeveless jacket called a *chupen*. Hair was long, and hats wide-brimmed. Feast-day clothes had pearl and silver buttons and were richly embroidered. The embroideries, also seen on the women's feast-day clothes, were worked in yellow and deep orange silk, and the patterns were like those of the stonework of castles and cathedrals of Brittany. One feast-day headdress for women in Quimper is called a *coif*: this is a stiff white cap with a lace over-cap, both worn over a little cap.

In Pont Avens in Lower Brittany the under-coif has blue streamers at the back, and there are wide lace wings curving out and over into the top of the coif. The bodice is embroidered with beadwork flowers

Festival dress of Pont Avens in Lower Brittany

Lace cap and 'collarette'

Festival dress of Plougastel, Brittany

Lace cornet of Brittany

Lace cap of Vannes, southern Brittany

Bourgoin of Normandy

Cap of the Pas de Calais region

and has a goffered muslin collar curving up at the shoulders. In nearby fishing villages women wear little net caps with stiff bows at the back and with lacy brims, which are sometimes made long and pinned up to make a *cornet*. In the eastern regions, the lace caps are flatter, like the cap from Vannes. The Vannes lace patterns are very beautiful and the black of the bodice helps to show off the creamy lace of kerchief and apron.

In the north-west of Brittany in Plougastel, the men's best clothes are gay with many coloured embroideries, and the women wear a headdress of two little under-caps with folded and pinned lace on top.

Normandy in northern France is famed for its lace and for the lacy tower headdresses called *bourgoins*. They are made from starched muslin over stiffened shapes and have velvet chin straps and lace stream-ers or wings. Feast-day dress for women includes lace shawls, hang-ing pockets, and jewellery.

From the Pas de Calais area op-posite the Kentish coast, comes the

Folk dancers of Bordeaux

fisherwoman's headdress of a cap with a frill starched and pleated into a halo, and with tiny lappets at each side. The dress is unusual in being highwaisted.

South of Brittany is the wine-growing region of Bordeaux. Here the girl's square-necked, striped dress is short, with sleeves gathered at the sides; the mob cap has a short frill, and the cap part is full and starched to make a halo. The man wears a beret, a striped, round-necked waistcoat, and a sash. Both men and women wear *espadrilles* (light canvas shoes with rope soles), which are tied on with laces. The *sabots* worn on the farm could be slipped on over the *espadrilles*, as in other parts of southern France.

Along the frontier with Spain lie the Pyrenees, high mountains with long deep valleys, where towns are built on rocky heights and where each valley has its own costume. In the Vallée de Campan in the east the women wear a scarlet capulet over a white cap, a full skirt, hand-woven in stripes, and an apron with appliqué flowers on the pockets. Men wear large flat berets, dark trousers and red sashes. Their jackets are knitted and have flowers embroidered on the front. As in other parts of southern France, they have a woollen cord finished with tassels or pompoms for a tie. *Espadrilles* are worn; or the pointed *sabots* often seen in the Pyrenees—the grander the occasion, the higher the points.

In the Vallée de Bethmale men wear little round caps, buff-coloured knitted jackets, loose, blue breeches with scarlet braiding, and a wide sash. They have loose buttoned gaiters, like those often worn by the shepherds of the region. Girls wear blue or striped skirts and scarlet aprons, embroidered bodices and lace or flower-patterned kerchiefs, and a white cap beneath a black embroidered coif with long streamers.

Amongst the folk costumes of Provence in the south of France the two most interesting are those of Brignoles and Arles. The women in the little village of Brignoles wear low-crowned black hats over their attractive goffered caps, and richly patterned skirts and aprons. Women from the old city of Arles wear long plain skirts, white lace fichus and tiny coifs tied round with black velvet ribbon whose ends are stiffened to stick out behind. Most of the Provençal men's costumes are forgotten, but red or blue sashes, and berets or wide-brimmed hats are worn for folk-dancing and some fishermen still wear red stocking caps.

Further to the north, the province of Bourbonnais is noted for its hats; one is the ornate straw topper with black velvet ribbons, which is worn over a lace cap, and another is the "*chapeau à deux bonjours*" (hat of two "good-days"). The brim of the "*chapeau à deux bonjours*" is raised at the front for the "*bonjour de devant*" (good-day from in front), and at the back for the "*bonjour de derrière*" (good-day from behind). It is made of straw and has black velvet ribbons and straw decorations.

22

Festival dress of the Pyrenees

Vallée de Campan

Vallée de Bethmale

Festival dress of Provence

Brignoles

Arles

Best dress of the province of Bourbonnais

It is lined with red for girls and with blue for older women and widows.

From Bazas, inland from Bordeaux, come the peasant group (see p. 26), the boy in a blue smock rather like those still worn by workmen all over France, the old man in a long sheepskin coat, and the girl in her wide-sleeved Sunday dress, small frilled apron and lacy fichu. Shawls are worn by the women, and big hats, which are put on over the cap to look like a great halo.

The northern province of Burgundy is another region where the women used to wear spectacular hats. The couple from Bourg-en-Bresse (see the left of p. 25) are going to a baptism. The man wears a smock, trousers, *sabots* and a stocking cap. The woman wears a wide-brimmed hat with a tiny, high crown. The girl from Tournus on the right wears a similar hat over a lacy cap; the bunch of ribbons on top is called a *brelot*.

Alsace, the most easterly province of France, is separated from Germany by the river Rhine. It has often been fought over and occupied by either France or Germany, and to preserve their identity in the confusion the Alsatian people have become an independent "nation". Their unity is shown in their folk costume, for the style of one or two regions has been generally adopted and might almost be called a true "national" costume. There are many feast-days to celebrate harvesting, and folk costumes are still worn on these occasions.

Sunday dress of Burgundy

Festival dress of Alsace

*Sunday dress of Bazas
in Guyenne*

The women's full skirts, which have two bands of velvet or brocade near the hem, are green for Protestants, red for Catholics, and mauve for Jewish women. The black bodice is laced over an embroidered *plastron* (ornamental panel) and a lacy fichu is tucked into it; a shawl may be draped round the shoulders. Aprons are embroidered with flowers, often white on black or black on white, and white knitted stockings are worn. The headdress is spectacular but simple: a small, fitting cap tied on top with an immense butterfly bow of wide ribbon, red for Catholics and black for Protestants.

The men wear black or dark suits with short jackets, red waistcoats, white shirts with stand-up collars, and white knitted socks. They wear fur caps or flat black hats. The chief feature of the men's costume is the use of gold buttons, two rows each on the waistcoat and on the jacket, three buttons on each trouser pocket, a row on the outside of each trouser leg, as well as others on the pockets and lapels.

Lace coif and heavily embroidered bodice of Finisterre, Brittany

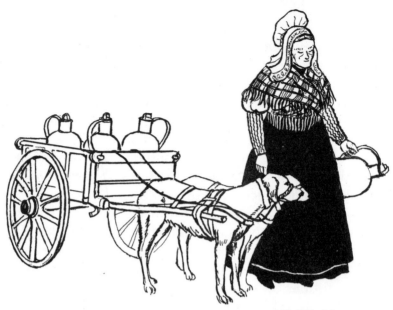

*Old Flemish woman
with her dog-cart*

3   Belgium

While some of the folk costumes of the Dutch Netherlands are still worn, very little survives of those of the Flemish and Walloon people in Belgium. The only folk costume worn by folk dancers consists of a peaked cap and blue smock for the men, and a full, accordion-pleated skirt for the women, which is worn with a Paisley shawl and a lace cap with long lappets. In the Walloon country in the east of Belgium the men's smock is pleated, and the women wear a bonnet instead of a cap. *Sabots* are still worn in country districts.

The historic cities of Flanders, where in medieval and Renaissance times artists and craftsmen worked, are renowned for their buildings, lace, tapestries, fine cloth, jewellery, paintings—for all these, and more.

The Guilds of the various trades and the fraternities that were responsible for defending the cities still hold their annual festivals, with traditional dances and processions, for which many different costumes are worn, some historic and some Carnival costumes with grotesque heads representing legendary figures. There are at least twenty-eight such festivals, some solemn and religious, others lively, with fireworks and dancing in the streets. A famous dance is that of the *Gilles*, or clowns, at Binche; the *Gilles* all wear Carnival dress, with sixteenth-century ruffs and huge plumed headdresses.

Festival dress of the
Walloon country, Belgium
    Centre: a Gilles in yellow and red, with lace
    collar, plumed headdress, and bells on his belt

4 The Netherlands

Although in the Netherlands there are big cities, modern industry and up-to-date farming, there are places where old customs linger on and folk costume is everyday wear. The people in the south and east have for centuries been farmers and fishers, dressing up for saints' days and festivals, and it is mostly there that the old costumes are found.

In the north and west are the polders, the lands reclaimed from the sea, and there many people are descended from the strict Puritans who had little time for revels. When the peasants of Friesland in the north dressed up, they adopted the costume of the rich gentry and burghers, which was worn for special occasions until early in this century. The men wore black suits with velvet breeches, top hats, and silver buttons and buckles. The women wore silk dresses, often patterned with flowers, aprons and kerchiefs or shawls of fine hand-made lace, and big embroidered hanging pockets. Under the lace caps, which had full frills at the back, were fitting caps made of real gold with two ornate gold pins at the forehead. This festival costume, which was intended to show off the wealth of the wearer, contrasts strongly with the practical workaday clothes of other regions.

The Netherlands are wet, and the wind and rain blow in from the sea, so the clothes of fisherfolk and peasants were full and heavy to keep them warm, and dark in colour. To make up for these sombre colours men wore silver buttons and pins for best, and the women gold orna-ments and necklaces of several strands of coral beads—it had to be real coral—fastened with gold or silver clasps. They also wore white caps of many different styles, often decorated with lace and drawn-thread

Festival dress of the
people of Friesland

Lace caps of Zeeland
and Walcheren

Sunday dress of Volendam in Holland

work, for best. Some of these can still be seen at Beveland in the western island of Zeeland. Here a big starched lace coif is worn over a white cap, which in turn is worn over a gold cap. On to this gold cap or gold framework are fixed the gold pins and the shiny gold plates that support the edge of the coif. The coif is round for Catholics and square for Protestants. Men wore two silver clasps at their collars, and two larger filigree clasps at the waistband.

The women's caps in Volendam on the Zuider Zee are pointed like medieval hoods, and have pointed turned-back wings. The rest of the dress is heavy; a big warm apron made with a strip of bright material at the top, a full skirt over several petticoats (at one time women wore a padded roll round their hips to throw the skirt out even further), and a fitting top with lace or embroidery for best. The men's costume has full trousers with silver buttons at the waistband, a short jacket, and always a cravat, even in summer, with a silver brooch on the right of the jacket collar and a silver chain on the left. A man engaged to be married used to wear a green ribbon in his cap, and several green bows on his wedding day.

The men's costume on the island of Marken is still worn for everyday. The men's breeches are wide at the top, and narrow at the knee so that seaboots can easily be worn over them.

All children in Marken used to dress alike until they were six, so the boy in the picture below wears a skirt and apron like his sister, but his hair is short, and there are no flowers on his bodice. Girls used

Family in best dress on the island of Marken

to have five flowers embroidered on their bodices until they were grown up, when they could have seven. Then, too, the bodice could be buttoned at the front and the woman's cap, which consisted of three bonnets worn one above the other on a stiffened frame, could be worn. Young girls wore a little lace cap, with an embroidered bonnet over it for out-of-door wear. The traditional Marken hairstyle is a long ringlet on each side of the face and a curled-up fringe, but many girls have short hair now.

Clogs, called *klompen*, are still worn in the Netherlands, as they are useful for outdoor work, and can be slipped on easily over thick knitted stockings or cloth inner shoes. Each region has its own style, as in France, so that you can tell by the *klompen* where a person comes from. A suitable dance costume for many folk dances of the Netherlands is worn by the pair below. It is like the costume worn by folk-dancing teams from the Netherlands for clog dances and, apart from the clogs, it is easy to make.

Dutch children dancing the old dance called Driekusman

5   Western Germany

Like France, Germany was once a number of kingdoms and principalities, which had their own courts and customs. Some of their fashions can still be seen in the folk costumes of present-day Germany. Some of the peasant costumes are worn for special occasions, while older fashions and Carnival costume can be seen at the Guild festivals and Carnivals.

Left: Gutachtal child's black lace bonnet with bead embroidery
Right: Gutachtal family in Sunday dress

In the south in the little villages among the trees of the Black Forest folk costumes are sometimes still worn. The men's best dress is generally rather like that which is worn in the village of Gutachtal: long or short coats, contrasting waistcoats, round, broad-brimmed hats, neckerchiefs, and plenty of buttons. The women wear fitting bodices over full-sleeved chemises (blouses), full skirts, and a variety of head-dresses. The Gutachtal bodice has an embroidered neckband and a square inset of patterned or embroidered material called a *Halsmantel*. The girl wears a fine black lace cap, with a black lace bow, often embroidered with beads at the back. Her mother wears a *Bollenhut*, a straw hat with pompoms which are red for young women and black for older ones; the more pompoms, the more important is the wearer. In other parts of the Black Forest, black headdresses were worn only by married women, and were called *Jochhauben*, which means "yoke-hoods". This showed that the wife had taken the yoke on her shoulders and would work in her husband's fields as well as his house.

The women of Elztal wear large top hats made of fine straw, lac-quered scarlet. In Villingen they wear haloes called "maidens' caps", *Mädelskappen*. These are made of thread woven on wire, in gold or silver for girls and in black for older women, and there are bows and

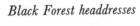

Black Forest headdresses

Topper of Elztal

Bridesmaid's Schappel

Mädelskappe from Villingen

Berchtesgarten region of the Bavarian Alps

streamers at the back. The *Schappel* is a crown of metal and wire decorated with glass, beads, jewels, and bits of mirror; in the middle is a bush on a wire framework, which is also decorated, mostly with real or artificial flowers, leaves and fruit. Crowns like these are worn in other parts of Europe, sometimes for church processions, but mostly for weddings. New ones are still made in the Black Forest, but many families have one as an heirloom. No one knows how old is the custom of wearing a bridal crown of flowers and fruit.

In the Bavarian Alps in the south-east, the men wear embroidered shorts and braces, sometimes made all of leather; in their hats they have a plume of hair from the chamois, the little deer of the mountains. In the past, they used to wear calf-socks without feet to them, knitted in coloured patterns. The women have silver laces and ornaments on

Vierland, Germany

Dance dress of Schwal[m]
in Hesse, central Germ[any]

Festival dress of
Schaumburg-Lippe in the north-west

The back, showing
the streamers and
huge brocade bow

Brooch and
embroidery

their bodices and wear round hats, often decorated with an eagle's feather. Green is a favourite colour, and many clothes are made of a thick, green, home-spun, showerproof cloth called *Loden.*

This elegant costume (see p. 37) contrasts strongly with others, such as the costume from the Schwalm valley in Hesse in central Germany (see p. 38). The skirt is short and very full, especially over the hips and at the back. It is worn over a padded roll tied round the middle, which makes the waist seem higher than the normal waistline. Many petticoats are worn, and the undermost one is very narrow, as it was in the days when the Hessian dances were very wild and the girls were turned upside down. The hair is twisted up into a tiny headdress with long ribbons.

Further to the north is Schaumburg-Lippe, once a tiny principality. From here comes a festival dress which is composed of a mixture of bygone fashions. The woman's dress has a fitting bodice and full skirt, a style that was worn all over Europe about four or five hundred years ago. Over it is a shawl of later fashion, and over this a lace ruff like those seen in seventeenth-century paintings. Over a little, fitting coif the woman wears a stiff black *hennin*—a headdress fashion from the Middle Ages—with long streamers at the back. Her gold earrings and heavy jewelled collar are like those worn more than a thousand years ago, and her round brooch is like brooches which have been found in Celtic burial places.

The girl from Vierlande in Lüneburg in the north wears a short jacket, showing her ornamental waistband, which is made of several bands of embroidery or braiding. Her apron is gathered into a band of another colour. She has a round straw hat over a small black cap with a stiff black bow at the back, which is tied with the ends sticking out. The man wears a great many buttons on his clothes, and he has a big patch sewn on to each sleeve to look like the cuff of a soldier's jacket.

Insel Förh is a German island in the North Sea near Denmark. Here dress is heavy to give protection against storms, and in dark, practical colours. The women used to wear a two-scarf headdress, as did others living on the North Sea coast. On feast-days they wore an embroidered tiara-like scarf, and an elaborate silver-laced breastwork of filigree silver with silver ball-buttons; in the nearby Halligen area, the breast-work was decorated with silver medallions.

*Filigree silver
ball-button*

*Breastwork of Föhr
with silver ball-buttons*

*Festival dresses of the German islands
of Föhr and Hallingen in the North Sea*

Embroidery motif of Falster

Festival dress of North Falster

6 Denmark

Not long ago, folk costume was worn every day in Denmark, even near cities and big sea-ports. Sunday and festival dresses were brightly coloured: blue for Christmas, green for Easter and red for Whitsun. Buttons and buckles were of silver or amber, and married women were allowed to leave the third bodice button undone. Costumes have many ribbons and ornamental bands, either woven or braided. Braiding is an ancient craft; a hair-net found in a Bronze Age burial mound was made of braids as still made by some Danish country women. The costume from the island of Falster in the south has many ribbons and braids. The dress is made of flowered material, and the summer bonnet has a brim of starched lace. The old fisherwoman (see p. 42) comes from Laesø, an island in the Kattegat between Denmark and Sweden. She wears a wimple, a headdress made from a length of white cloth, like those worn in the Middle Ages. Her silver chain with its dangling

Festival dress with silver ornaments and solid silver belt: Danish island of Laesø

ornaments, and her silver studded belt are of a much older fashion. Ornaments like these were found in Viking and Bronze Age burial places. Only married women in Laesø were allowed to wear silver, and since there were no silver mines on the island girls used to make a long voyage and overland journey, called "fetching silver", to buy it for their weddings.

Along the North Sea coast clothes were heavy. Fanø is a place of sand-dunes, and when the gales from the sea blew up the sand the women wore a mask called a *strud*. They wore full skirts, red for married women and green for girls, and big aprons which were almost like another skirt.

Aprons are an important part of women's costume all over Denmark. They were always worn, even for best. In the past there were wolves in Denmark, and people told stories of the phantom Werewolf. Aprons were said to protect their wearers from the Werewolf, and this old legend has taken so long to die out that even in the nineteen-thirties a countrywoman confessed to wearing her apron underneath her modern dress.

Sunday dress of Fanø and of Rømø
with silver ball-buttons on the bodice
The child is wearing a strud

Festival dress from Hedebo near Odense

The neckerchief was another item commonly worn. In Fanø it was worn with the point at the front and with the ends crossed over at the back. The headdress was complicated: first a folded white kerchief was put over the head, and pinned at the back; then a cap stuffed with horsehair; then a larger kerchief matching the neckerchief; and lastly another kerchief tied on the top with the right hand end pointing forward, and the left hand end sticking up. This sort of double kerchief headdress was common in villages all along the North Sea coast, not only in Denmark, as it was practical in cold windy weather.

Seamen from the fishing villages when ashore, usually dressed like townsmen. Anyone who had crossed the Equator could wear a distinguishing yellow silk waistcoat.

Hedebo, near Odense, is very famous for its embroidery, which can be seen on the costume illustrated. The girl's headdress is unusual for

she wears a scarf tied over her bonnet. The man wears a longish waistcoat, a long jacket and a stocking cap. The man of Odense on p. 45
is wearing a striped waistcoat.

Many women's folk costumes in Scandinavia have accordion-pleated
skirts, as do the costumes of many other regions. Danish women called
this pleating "cooked" pleating, because the material, after being
carefully pleated and wrapped in damp muslin, was put into the oven
as it was cooling after baking, so that the pleats would be set by the
heat. In Denmark, the pleats were fairly wide, and in Sweden very
narrow.

Apart from clogs which are useful on the farm and which people still
wear in the summer, folk costume in Denmark is now worn only for
folk-dancing. Some of these costumes are family heirlooms, and some
are specially made by craftswomen.

Best dress of Odense   *A family on Sunday in Himmerland*

Folk costume of different parts of Sweden

Vånga

Skedevi

Blekinge

Winter clothes
of Delsbo

Married woman
of Blekinge

Delsbo

7 Sweden

Embroidery of Hälsingland, Sweden

There are a great many folk costumes in Sweden, and each has its own history, often so old as to be forgotten. The costume from Vonga, a village in Östergotland (East Gotland) has full white trousers and a long straight coat rather like the old medieval dress. The round cap, made of wool or leather, is so old a style that no one can trace when it started. The leather apron is worn, not for work, but for special occasions; the reason for this, too, is lost in the past. The woman from nearby Skedevi wears an unusual headdress, a starched square folded diagonally and tied with the right end pointing down, and the left up.

When folk costume was everyday wear, each village was very particular to see that its own costume was not altered, and newcomers to the village had to adopt it. There has been civil war in Sweden in the past, and costumes may have been a way of telling friend from foe.

Clothes were made from hand-spun and hand-woven woollen cloth, dyed with vegetable dyes; fine clothes were richly embroidered. During the winter, the women worked at embroidering while the men were busy with leather work and wood-carving. Many families have a folk costume, often for a child, as an heirloom.

The southern province of Blekinge is called the "garden of Sweden". One of the Blekinge costumes opposite has a special headdress for unmarried women, red with coloured ribbons, while the married women, who must not show their hair, wear a specially folded white square. The girl has stockings knitted in red, black and white wool, and like many other Swedish girls, she wears her shawl tucked inside her bodice.

47

Costume of Dalecarlia

Wooden horse of Dalecarlia

Little boy of Skäne   Best dress of Rättvik   Unmarried woman

Rättvik is in Dalecarlia, the "heart of Sweden". Although there are modern industrial towns near by, in the country many people still wear folk costume for special occasions and on Sundays, when the old Church Boats still bring people to church across the lakes. Here again, married women wear white headdresses, and single girls coloured caps. Dress and apron are sometimes made in one, the skirt of the dress being accordion pleated. The knitted stockings used to be worn full at the ankle, to show that the wearer was well off. The strong leather shoes, like others in Sweden, had birch bark in the soles for extra strength. The man's flat hat with its red pompoms and his straight jacket were adapted from Renaissance fashions.

48

In Delsbo in the more northerly region of Gävleborg girls wear their hair loose, which is unusual. Also unusual are the forked tongues of women's shoes. The woman wears a jacket knitted in coloured patterns, and her cap is embroidered. The man's costume has an abundance of buttons, a round cap, and knee-bands of woollen cloth with leather studs. For winter, the man wears a long coat and a knitted cap (see p. 46).

The headdress from Bara in the southern fishing region of Skäne dates from the Middle Ages. It is a white kerchief pinned over a kidney-shaped support. The embroidered cap illustrated comes from Leksands Noret, another Dalecarlian village where folk costume is still worn. The third cap comes from the western region of Värmland. Embroidered hanging pockets in a different design for each parish are worn, according to Swedish custom, half under the apron.

Cap of Värmland

Embroidered cap and pocket of Leksands Noret in Dalecarlia

Headdress of Bara in Skäne

Left: Embroidered Norwegian glove
Right: Ancient Viking necklace
and a traditional brooch

8 Norway

The folk costume of Norway is said to be the most elegant in Europe. There is rich embroidery on best clothes; some of it is in coloured thread on the woollen cloth of suits and dresses, and some of it is "whitework" similar to the drawn thread work and needle-weaving done in the Hardanger Fjord in the west. Intricate and beautiful patterns are worked into practical, simple garments. The gold and silver jewellery is similar to that of the Norwegians' Viking ancestors. The colours are so well chosen, and so well set off by the fair colouring of the people, that the costumes never seem over-decorated, and all sorts of styles are harmoniously blended.

The farming province of Telemark in the east has some of the most spectacular costumes of Norway. Jumpers are knitted in coloured patterns for women, and in black and white for men. Many of the men's garments are also black and white, for instance, their short white jackets with black embroidery and silver buttons. The girl (below) from Heddal ("dal" in Norwegian means "valley") in East Telemark also wears a short jacket, which is red and fastened at the side. She has a broad woven belt, and her apron is embroidered with *Rosesom*, the rose embroidery found especially in Telemark, but also in other parts of Norway. Her headband, that of a single girl, is of braided wool. The other woman (below left) wears the headdress of married women in her part of Telemark, and also the *solje*, the large "sun" brooch, often an heirloom, which is given to a girl on her wedding day.

Married woman and man of western Telemark   *Girl of eastern Telemark*

The costume of Setesdal in the south shows details of many fashions. The men are said to be among the tallest in Europe, and because of their fine build they used to join European armies as mercenary soldiers. They brought home from abroad ideas for their unusual clothes. Jackets and waistcoats were worn very short; they and the bibs to the trousers are blue or black and heavily embroidered. The leather patches on the trousers are said to come from the uniform of the Spanish cavalry. A silver chain and clasp were worn to fasten the jacket.

The girl's short jacket is fastened with silver chains. She wears a short skirt over a long underskirt; both are made to stand out by the stiff braiding round the edge.

Festival dress of Setesdal

Festival dress of Hallingdal near Oslo

Girl of Voss, west Norway

The long valley of Hallingdal, which runs for many miles into the country north-west of Oslo, is known for its music and energetic dances. The costume is fittingly bright: the men wear green waistcoats, embroidered breeches of the older, fuller type, black and white knitted stockings and round caps. The women's dresses are high-waisted or have no waist at all. The blouses are embroidered in white. For weekdays a belt used to be worn, and a dark jacket for out of doors.

From Voss in the west comes the costume (above right) with the white headkerchief called a *skaut*, embroidered in Voss "blackwork" (embroidery in black thread) and pinned at the back. The bodice has an embroidered plastron and the belt is studded with brass.

Many families have a folk dress as an heirloom, and some girls, like the one from Gudbrandsdal (below), make and embroider one for themselves. In all the Scandinavian countries, Denmark, Sweden, Finland and Norway, winter is cold and dark, and the people used to spend the long hours when they had to stay indoors at skilled handicrafts: leatherwork, carving, silverwork, weaving and embroidery. The Scandinavian governments now encourage people to keep up these old skills, and so beautiful hand-made articles can still be bought, including the folk costumes.

Folk dancers take great care to wear the correct costumes for their dances. The Hardanger costume is shown below, where the people are dancing the *Kyndletanz* or Torch dance, which was always danced at weddings in the old days.

Left: mother and daughter of Gudbrandsdal
Centre: child of Hardanger
Right: married couple of Hardanger
The wife is wearing a skaut

Best dress of Säkylän in western Finland

9   Finland

The people of Finland, the "country of six thousand lakes", are not of the same stock as the rest of the Scandinavian peoples. They have their own language, music, legends, customs.

However, for over six hundred years, Finland was a province of Sweden, and the costumes of western Finland are like those of Sweden. The couple from Säkylän in the west (shown above) wear full-sleeved blouses, and the man has many silver buttons while the woman wears a beautiful silver necklace. Married women, according to old custom, can leave all but the last two buttons of their bodices undone. The stripes on the woman's skirt and bodice are woven into the material; those of the skirt are blue, red, yellow, and green. Green is a favourite colour in Finland. Each village used to have its own stripe pattern, and the stripes were always vertical. The man's striped waistcoat, short jacket and knee-bands are in Swedish style, but the high shirt collar with a narrow neckband fastened with a brooch is typical of Finland.

Later, Finland became a part of the Empire of the Russian Tsars. The eastern provinces of Karelia and the Karelian isthmus are now in Russia, and some of the garments there have a Russian look. But these regions are remote, so it is not surprising to find that the styles of basic garments date back to the Middle Ages and before. The loose coat of the man from Jääski in Karelia (below) could be made of sheepskin or of the white woollen material which was used for the cloaks that were worn not long ago. With his traditional loose coat

Costume of Karelia, eastern Finland

Silver brooch

Birch bark shoes

Jääski

Seiskarin

Karelian headdresses

Zoutseno

Rauden

the man wears a nineteenth-century top hat, and soft leather shoes, like moccasins. The man from Seiskarin (see p. 56) has a loose jacket tied with thongs, skin boots with knee-bands of studded leather, and the ancient round cap. Shoes were often woven from birch bark, according to old custom.

The woman from Jääski (opposite) wears a medieval wimple, a white kerchief over a support. The white headdress from Zoutseno is also medieval. Other headdresses were like that of Rauden, with a front decorated with stiff embroidery or a woven pattern, and with an extended and patterned neck-frill. The headdress was tied at the nape of the neck. Such headdresses were worn in some places until this century. Unmarried girls wore different types of headband.

Metal belt with hanging
knife, key and purse

Girl from Tuuteri

Bead-embroidered head-band

The girl from Tuuteri, now in Soviet Karelia, wears a band of red wool with metal studs. Her blouse has a plastron of richly patterned woven material. Skirts are of plain, dark material with coloured borders.

In parts of eastern Finland, some women's costumes included a belt from which hung a sheath knife for defence, as well as a needle-case and purse. The belts were often made of metal, or of studded leather, like the belts worn by Teutonic women as early as A.D. 400. The round brooches worn by the women are often heirlooms of ancient design. Such brooches have been found in Bronze Age burial places in Finland.

58

Lapp family

10 Lapland

Lapland is the most northerly part of Scandinavia, stretching across from northern Norway and Sweden into northern Russia. It is a country of continuous daylight at midsummer, and continuous dark at midwinter. Many people, especially sailors, used to think of it as a place of mystery and magic.

Like the Finns, the Lapps are of an ancient race, unlike other Scandinavian peoples. They follow the reindeer herds which are their

Cap of the Four Winds

livelihood. Until recently, they always wore their traditional costume, but now they are beginning to wear modern, factory-made clothing.

In winter men and women wear a reindeer-skin tunic called a *peski*, with the hair inside for warmth, skin trousers, and soft leather shoes or boots. Inside the boots they pack a special rushy grass which is warm in winter and cool in summer. Under their tunics are shirts and knitted jerseys, and on their feet woollen stockings. A cape is worn in very cold weather.

In the summer the costume is much the same, but made of woollen cloth. Bands of brightly coloured cloth, chiefly red and yellow, are sewn on to the tunics, which are tied with plaited woollen cords. The hard nomadic life used not to leave time for embroidery, but nowadays the white shirts are sometimes embroidered. There is much decoration on the leather belts worn by both men and women, and on the reindeer harnesses. Leather shoes and boots are decorated, and the stockings are knitted in two or more bright colours.

The women wear bright aprons, long-fringed shawls and lace caps, with warm red caps for outdoors. Babies are firmly swaddled and tied into big cradles made of light wooden frames covered with reindeer skin, which the mother carries with her wherever she goes. The coloured beads on the cradle were originally put there to keep off evil spirits: now they are a traditional decoration.

Men wear peaked caps with huge red pompoms, like that of the boy on p. 59. An older version of the cap is the "Cap of the Four Winds", so called because of its four long points. Unmarried men wear the cap with all the points to the front, and add to its decorations of coloured braids a knot of coloured ribbons.

The Lapp costume is one of the most ancient costumes of western Europe. Because Lapland is so remote, it has not been exposed to the changes in fashion of other countries. But even if it had been, it is unlikely that it would have changed greatly, for the conditions of weather and of the Lapps' way of life control the simple forms of dress, making the Lapps' folk costume a strictly practical one.

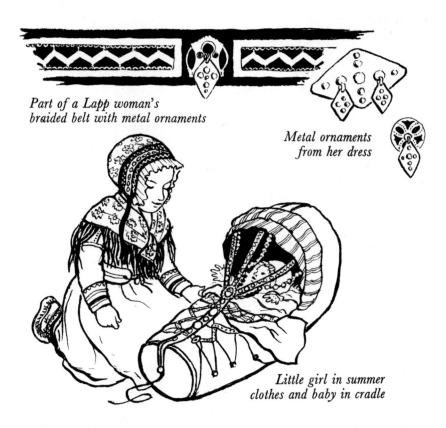

Part of a Lapp woman's braided belt with metal ornaments

Metal ornaments from her dress

Little girl in summer clothes and baby in cradle

SHETLAND
ISLANDS

ORKNEY
ISLANDS

SCOTLAND

NORTH
SEA

Connemara

IRELAND

Munster

WALES

ENGLAND

London

NORWAY

Oslo

SWEDEN

LAPLAND

KARELIA

FINLAND

RUSSIA

BALTIC SEA

DENMARK

HOLLAND

GERMANY
WEST   EAST

BELGIUM

River Rhine

Bavarian Alps

NORMANDY

BRITTANY

FRANCE

ALSACE

SWITZER-
LAND

AUSTRIA

ITALY

Bordeaux

Arles

PROVENCE

PYRENEES

SPAIN

1
2
3
4
5
6
7
8
9
10
11
12
13
14
15
16
17
18
19
20
21
22
23
24
25
26
27
28
29
30
31
32
33
34
35
36
37
38
39
40
41
42
43
44
45
46
47

Key to Map

Index